**THINGS YOU DIDN'T**

Republic of
KOREA

**Written and Illustrated
by Sean O'Neill**

Egremont, Massachusetts

50 Things You Didn't Know About is produced and published by Red Chair Press:
www.redchairpress.com

FREE lesson guide at www.redchairpress.com/free-activities

Publisher's Cataloging-In-Publication Data

(Provided by Cassidy Cataloging Services, Inc)

Names: O'Neill, Sean, 1968- author, illustrator. | O'Neill, Sean, 1968 50 things you didn't know about (Series)

Title: 50 things you didn't know about Republic of Korea / written and illustrated by Sean O'Neill.

Other Titles:Republic of Korea

Description: Egremont, Massachusetts : Red Chair Press, [2024] | Interest age level: 006-009. | Includes bibliographical references and index. | Summary: With 50 Things You Didn't Know About Republic of Korea, young readers will discover highlights of Korea's ancient cultures, its modern traditions and discover unique aspects of food, industry and daily life in the highly modern nation known as South Korea.--Publisher.

Identifiers: ISBN: 978-1-64371-354-0 (library hardcover) | 978-1-64371-355-7 (softcover) | 978-1-64371-356-4 (ebook) | LCCN: 2023936981

Subjects: LCSH: Korea (South)--History--Juvenile literature. | Korea (South)--Description and travel-- Juvenile literature. | Korea (South)--Social life and customs--Juvenile literature. | CYAC: Korea (South)--History. | Korea (South)--Description and travel. | Korea (South)-- Social life and customs. | BISAC: JUVENILE NONFICTION / Travel. | JUVENILE NONFICTION / People & Places / Asia.

Classification: LCC: DS902 .O54 2024 | DDC: 951.95--dc23

Copyright © 2025 Red Chair Press LLC
RED CHAIR PRESS, the RED CHAIR and associated logos are registered trademarks of Red Chair Press LLC.

All rights reserved. No part of this book may be reproduced, stored in an information or retrieval system, or transmitted in any form by any means, electronic, mechanical including photocopying, recording, or otherwise without the prior written permission from the Publisher. For permissions, contact info@redchairpress.com

Printed in the United States of America

0524 1P F24CG

TABLE of CONTENTS

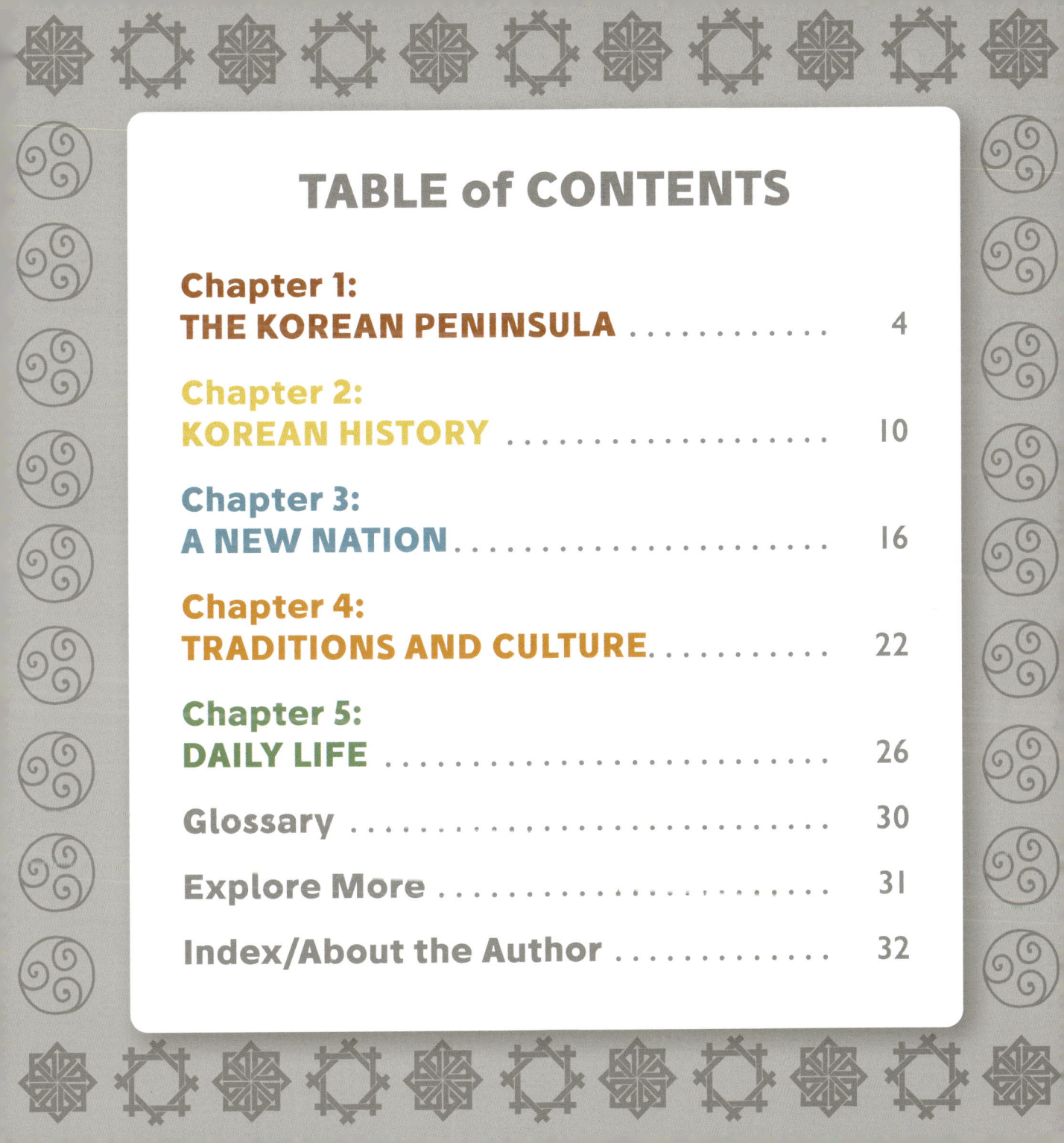

Chapter 1:
THE KOREAN PENINSULA 4

Chapter 2:
KOREAN HISTORY 10

Chapter 3:
A NEW NATION 16

Chapter 4:
TRADITIONS AND CULTURE 22

Chapter 5:
DAILY LIFE 26

Glossary 30

Explore More 31

Index/About the Author 32

CHAPTER 1

THE KOREAN PENINSULA

The mountainous strip of land that we call the Korean Peninsula has been home to the Korean people since the earliest settlers came south from the Mongolian plains about 5,000 years ago. Although much smaller than its neighbors China and Japan, this land has been home to one of the world's greatest and most unique societies.

THE KOREAN PENINSULA

1 South Korea is part of a landmass in East Asia called the Korean Peninsula. It's been said that the **peninsula** resembles a tiger, with its head and feet bordering China, and the rest of its body surrounded by ocean.

2 According to legend, Korea was founded by an ancient leader named Dangun. According to the story, Dangun's mother was a bear and he lived for more than 1,000 years before becoming a mountain god. The founding of Korea is celebrated every October 3 as National Foundation Day.

3 One of the most traditional symbols of Korea is the mighty Amur (or Siberian) tiger. Unfortunately, today it's only a symbol. These tigers have been extinct in Korea for many years.

4 Over the centuries, the people of the peninsula have had many names for their land. An early name was *Joseon*, which means "Land of the Morning Calm." Sounds like a nice place, but Korea's history hasn't always been calm.

THE KOREAN PENINSULA

5 The people of Korea have also been referred to by many names by their neighbors. One of these, the "People Who Wear White," refers to the traditional white robe, called a *hanbok*, that Koreans wore in the early kingdoms.

6 Bamboo plants are a symbol of loyalty and long life. Long ago, Koreans would plant bamboo trees to show their loyalty to the king.

7   Conservation of natural beauty has a long tradition in Korea. As far back as 500 CE, monks would guard the areas around their monasteries to protect the beauty of the environment.

8   The small island of Jeju off Korea's southern coast is home to many wild ponies. They are the descendants of ponies brought there by Mongolian invaders in the 14th century.

9   Jeju is just one of Korea's over 3,000 islands. If you decided to visit them all and spend a day on each, it would take about ten years.

THE KOREAN PENINSULA

10 At the base of Jeju island is *Yongduam*—Dragon Head Rock. According to legend, the rock is the remains of a giant dragon that angered a volcano spirit and was turned to stone. Only the head is visible, but when the tide goes out, his tail suddenly appears.

11 The island of Jeju is also known for the famous diving women of Jeju. These female fishers dive to the seabed for shellfish without any breathing tank. They can stay underwater for more than two minutes holding their breath!

CHAPTER 2

KOREAN HISTORY

Today South Korea constitutes the southern section of the peninsula, but starting about 700 CE the lands of the Korean people were united as one land, called the *Silla* kingdom. Over the centuries, other dynasties would take control, but the Korean national identity remained strong.

KOREAN HISTORY

12 An important figure from early Korean history was Queen Seondeok, who became the first woman to lead a united Korea. She's still remembered as a great leader, and a TV show based on her life was a huge hit on Korean television.

13 One of Queen Seondeok's great achievements was the creation of the *Cheomseongdae*, which is now the oldest **astronomical** observatory in the world. It was built out of 365 bricks—one for each day of the year.

14 Many great temples were built during the *Silla* period which featured huge bronze bells. The largest of these is the Divine Bell of King Seongdeok. It's said that the bell's ring can be heard 30 miles away.

15 The *Silla* dynasty was followed by the *Koguryo* dynasty, later renamed *Koryo*. This is where the name Korea comes from.

16 A major technological advance from this period was printing. The *Tripitaka Koreana* is an ancient religious document printed on 81,000 wood blocks in the 13th century.

17 Koreans also developed a system called *jikji*, in which different words can be printed using individual metal letterforms. This is the earliest known example of moveable type—about 100 years before Gutenberg's printing press.

KOREAN HISTORY

18 After the *Koryo* era came the *Joseon* dynasty in 1392. One of the great leaders from this period was King Sejong the Great, who ruled in the 15th century. His rule was marked by great advancements in technology and culture.

19 For many centuries the Korean language was only spoken—not written. Chinese invaders forced the Koreans to use Chinese characters for writing, but finally in the 15th century, King Sejong ordered the creation of *Hangeul*—the first and only Korean alphabet.

20 The first ironclad warships with metal protective armor were built in Korea in the 16th century. The great admiral Yi Sun-sin developed the technology, and the ships were nearly indestructible. They were called "turtle ships" because of their protective shell.

KOREAN HISTORY

21 For 200 years between 1640-1870, Korea was isolated from all other countries and cultures. During this period, they were referred to as "The Hermit Kingdom."

22 In 1653, a Dutch ship ran aground on Jeju. This was the first time in history that any European set foot in Korea.

23 The nearly 1,000 years of unified Korea came to an end in 1910, when Japan invaded. Korea would remain a Japanese colony until the end of World War II in 1945.

24 At the end of the war, Korea was divided down the middle by the Soviet Union and the allied forces of the U.S. and Great Britain. This separation led to the formation of two countries, and, soon after, the Korean War.

CHAPTER 3

A NEW NATION

In the wake of Japan's defeat in World War II, Korea's future was uncertain. The United Nations' plan for a united, democratic Korea wasn't supported by the Soviet Union, so, in August of 1948, elections were held in the south, and the first-ever government of the new Republic of Korea (the official name of South Korea) was formed. But years of conflict lay ahead for the new nation.

A NEW NATION

25 The Korean War lasted from 1950–1953, with the U.S. and its **allies** supporting South Korea, and China fighting with North Korea. The war was very destructive to both countries, and left the peninsula partitioned, or divided, as it remains today.

26 A cease-fire was called for in 1953, and an area was created between the two nations called the **demilitarized zone**, or DMZ. But a treaty was never signed, and, at least officially, the war still hasn't actually ended.

27 One unexpected outcome of partition is that the DMZ has become a habitat for wild animals. Because no people live there, and rarely enter into it, it's become a haven for migratory birds and other wildlife.

28 The South Korean flag is called the *Taegeukgi*. The *taegeuk* circle in the center represents balance between positive and negative forces in the universe. The four groups of lines around it represent the elements: heaven, earth, fire and water.

29 Because of centuries of cultural isolation, South Korea is not a diverse country. In fact, 99.9% of South Korean citizens are ethnically Korean, which means they trace their heritage back 5,000 years to the earliest inhabitants.

30 There are many Koreans outside of North and South Korea, however. Over 2 million Koreans live in the U.S. and almost a million live in Japan.

A NEW NATION

31 Many Korean families were separated during partition, and haven't seen each other since. In 1985, the first reunion was held and a small number of family members were allowed to see each other for the first time in decades.

32 The *currency*, or money, of South Korea is called the *won*. Each won is worth a lot less than a U.S. dollar. A pair of jeans costs about 80,000 won, and a hamburger is 4,000.

THE BLUE HOUSE

33 In the U.S. the president lives in the White House. In South Korea, it's the Blue House! The presidential residence got this name because of its distinctive blue tiled roof.

34 South Korea is crowded with 52 million people! The population density of the country is about 1,300 people per square mile. Compare that to the U.S., which has only about 96 people per square mile.

A NEW NATION

35 South Korea's capital city, Seoul, is even more crowded. So crowded, in fact, that the South Korean government decided to build a new capital city 100 miles away. The new city is under construction, and the new National Assembly should be open in 2027.

36 Seoul has grown so much that little remains of its ancient past. *Dongdaemun*, the Great East Gate, is one of the last remaining gates of the ancient city wall, and is now a tourist attraction.

CHAPTER 4

TRADITIONS AND CULTURE

Koreans of all types are deeply proud of their ancient traditions and unique cultural character. Because of centuries of isolation, the culture of Korea is unique among Asian nations, and unlike any other in the world. Some of these facts may help explain why.

TRADITIONS AND CULTURE

37 *Taekwondo*, translated as "the way of the hand and the foot," was created in Korea about 2,000 years ago. It is the oldest form of martial arts, and is now the national sport of South Korea.

38 Speaking of hand and foot, an unusual Korean art form is *baltal*, a form of puppet theater. It's similar to other forms of puppeteering, with one big difference: the puppeteers use their feet, not their hands.

39 Koreans celebrate birthdays a little differently than most people. All Koreans get one year older on New Year's Day, January 1. Birthdays are just a day for celebration.

40 Koreans celebrate a baby's 100th day of life. In ancient times, many babies didn't live this long. Today almost all do, but it is still a cause for celebration.

41 On the child's actual first birthday, there is a celebration called *dol*. The child is placed before a table filled with different items. Whatever the birthday baby grabs first will predict their future.

42 At a Korean wedding, it is traditional for families to give newlyweds a pair of wooden ducks.

TRADITIONS AND CULTURE

43 South Korea is home to many of the world's greatest cartoon animation studios. Episodes of *The Simpsons*, *Family Guy*, and *Phineas and Ferb* are all produced in Seoul.

44 In recent years, South Korean pop culture has taken the world by storm. K-pop music is hugely popular everywhere. The video for the 2011 hit song "Gangnam Style" has been viewed over 2 billion times online.

CHAPTER 5

DAILY LIFE

In the years after its founding, South Korea was an impoverished and largely rural society, but after The Korean War, the speed of South Korea's modernization and technical advancement was truly electrifying. Today, South Korean cities like Seoul are vibrant hubs of innovation where ancient tradition and dazzling technology live side by side.

DAILY LIFE

45 The Korean people are sometimes known as "The Courteous People of the East." Courtesy and polite behavior are very important to Koreans.

46 Most Koreans use an **ingenious** technology for heating their homes, which goes back over 1,000 years. The ancient Joseon developed a system called *ondol*, in which pipes from a furnace were run under a stone floor to heat the whole house from below. Most Korean homes are still heated this way.

47 The most popular food throughout Korea is undoubtedly *kimchi*. This dish of spicy pickled cabbage with other vegetables is generally served with every meal. In olden days families would make huge crocks of kimchi and store it outside all winter.

48 If you're getting your picture taken in Korea, be sure to smile. But don't say "cheese", say "kimchi!"

DAILY LIFE

49 South Koreans love to shop, so it's no wonder that the world's largest department store is located there. Shinsegae Centumcity Department Store in Seoul has over 3 million square feet for your shopping pleasure. That's more than 52 football fields in size!

50 Today South Korea is a highly technologically advanced society. They are at the forefront of using robots, not only in factories, but also as restaurant waiters and even as prison guards.

Glossary

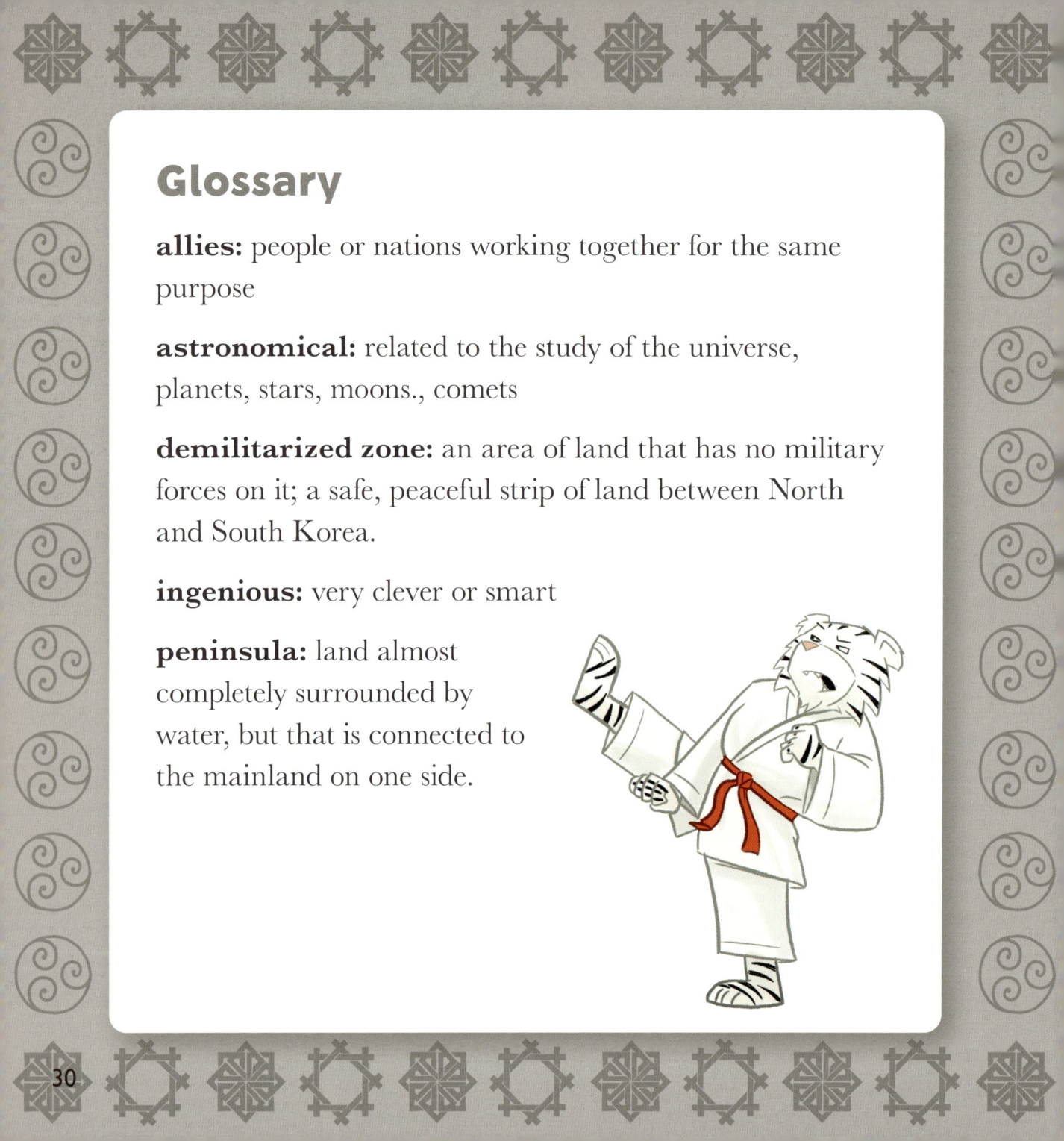

allies: people or nations working together for the same purpose

astronomical: related to the study of the universe, planets, stars, moons., comets

demilitarized zone: an area of land that has no military forces on it; a safe, peaceful strip of land between North and South Korea.

ingenious: very clever or smart

peninsula: land almost completely surrounded by water, but that is connected to the mainland on one side.

Explore More

Bowler, Ann Marie. *All About Korea*. Tuttle Publishing, 2018.

Dickman, Nancy. *Your Passport to South Korea*. Capstone Press, 2021.

Frisch-Schmoll, Joy. *Let's Look at North Korea*. Capstone Press, 2019.

Perkins, Chloe & Tom Wooley. *Living in South Korea (Ready to Read)*. Simon Spotlight, 2017.

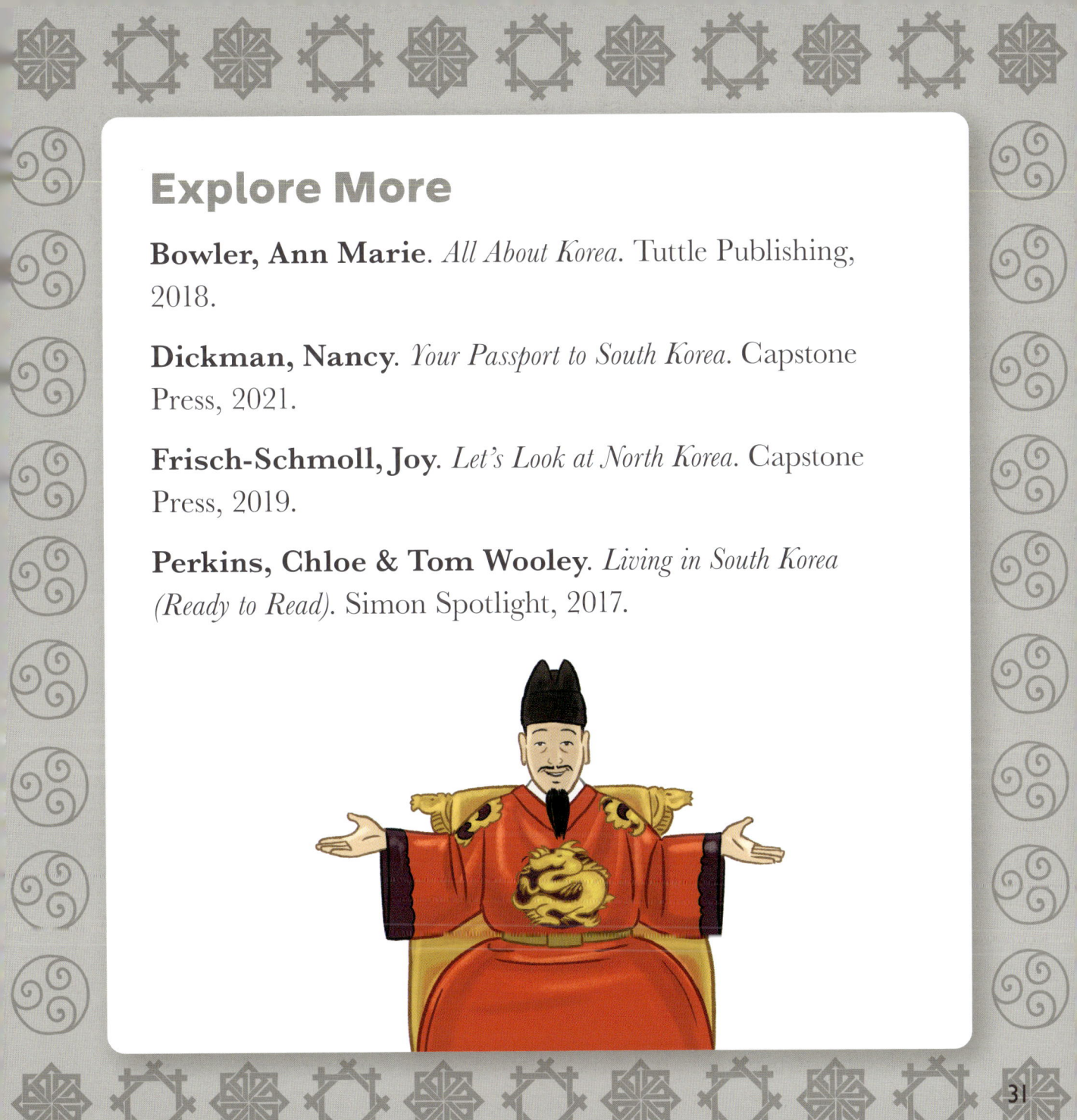

Index

bamboo	7	Korean War	17
Blue House	20	Koryo dynasty	12-13
China	5	Sejong, King	13
Dangun	5	Seondeok, Queen	11
DMZ	17	Seoul	21, 26
hanbok	7	Silla dynasty	12
Jeju	8-9, 15	Tae kwan do	23
Joseon	6, 13, 27	Yi Sun-sin, Admiral	14
kimchi	28	Yongduam	9

About the Author/Illustrator

Sean O'Neill is an illustrator and writer living in Chicago. He is the creator of *50 Things You Didn't Know* and the *Rocket Robinson* series of graphic novels. Sean loves history, trivia, and drawing cartoons, so this project is pretty much a dream assignment. Plus, he loves to preform Gangnam Style.